REVIVAL OF THE DRY BONES

REVIVAL OF THE DRY BONES

BILL VINCENT

CONTENTS

Disclaimer 1

1 Revival of the Dry Bones: A Call to Spiritual Awak 3

About the Author 20

Copyright © 2024 by Bill Vincent
All rights reserved. No part of this book may be reproduced in any manner whatsoever without written permission except in the case of brief quotations embodied in critical articles and reviews.
First Printing, 2024

Disclaimer

"I've transformed my sermons into book form. Please note that we've refined the content for clarity and a smoother reading experience. We trust you'll find it engaging."

CHAPTER 1

Revival of the Dry Bones: A Call to Spiritual Awak

I thank You, Lord, for what You're speaking to us. I thank You, Lord, for breaking off anything that is not of God. Cleanse this room as we prepare to preach, in Jesus' name. Hallelujah. Today, God led me to the book of Ezekiel and began to talk to me about the fire of God.

You might say, "Didn't we just talk about that?" Well, guess what—there's more fire. How many of you know we need more fire? These two need more fire. Let's turn to Ezekiel, chapter 37. If you've got time, or you can just write it down.

Chapter 37, verses 1 through 14:

"The hand of the Lord was upon me, and He carried me out in the Spirit of the Lord, setting me in the midst of a valley full of bones. He made me pass by them, all around them, and behold, there were very many in the open valley, and they were very dry.

He said to me, 'Son of man, can these bones live?' I answered, 'O Lord God, You know.' Again, He said to me, 'Prophesy over these bones and say to them, "O dry bones, hear the word of the Lord."'

In verse 5, it says, 'Thus says the Lord God to these bones: Behold, I will cause breath to enter into you, and you shall live. I will lay sinews on you, bring flesh upon you, and cover you with skin. I will put breath in you, and you shall live. Then you shall know that I am the Lord.'

So I prophesied as I was commanded. And as I prophesied, there was a noise, a rattling, and the bones came together, bone to bone. As I watched, sinews and flesh appeared on them, and skin covered them, but there was no breath in them. Then He said to me, 'Prophesy to the breath; prophesy, son of man, and say to the breath, "Thus says the Lord God: Come from the four winds, O breath, and breathe on these slain, that they may live."'

So I prophesied as He commanded me, and breath came into them, and they lived and stood upon their feet—an exceedingly great army. Then He said to me, 'Son of man, these bones are the whole house of Israel. They say, "Our bones are dry, our hope is lost, and we are cut off." Therefore, prophesy and say to them, "Thus says the Lord God: Behold, My people, I will open your graves and bring you up from them, and bring you into the land of Israel."'

Verse 13: 'Then you shall know that I am the Lord when I have opened your graves, O My people, and brought you up from your graves. I will put My Spirit in you, and you shall live. I will place you in your own land. Then you shall know that I, the Lord, have spoken and performed it,' says the Lord God."

I believe this is one of the most powerful messages that can be preached. God has given me two different directions with this, but I'm only going to take one tonight. The world is searching for God, let me tell you that. Right now, the world is desperately seeking God. Tragically and ironically, as the world seeks God, His people are asleep. Religious traditions are sleeping, while God looks at a world that needs Him and is searching for Him, and He sees a dead, sleeping church.

So, my question and comment tonight is this: It's time for revival. I'm not talking about the Azusa Street revival, or Toronto, or Pensacola, or any other revival we've been a part of. I'm talking about a revival that the world has never seen before.

The world wants and needs to know how to come to God and worship—not by man's opinion, but by what the Lord says. The world wants to hear what God is saying. People are anxious, waiting, and searching, but they're looking in the wrong places for answers right now. They're following leaders, but the problem is those leaders are demonic, leading them into darkness. The world needs models of authentic Christian living—people who can be a prototype of what God is about to do. The world wants to see God, and it's been longing for the Word of God, but what it has received has been empty of the information it truly needs.

You can't preach a watered-down gospel and expect everyone to be satisfied. What about the world's problems? As I said last night, God gave us a prescription on how to release His fire upon the church. You're not going to get it by offering candy-coated religion. You're not going to reach the church by preaching dead sermons. You have to preach the truth and address what's happening in our world right now. You can't just ignore it. You can have revival, you can have breakthrough, but you must make it relevant to today. Righteousness exalts a nation, but sin is a disgrace to any people.

How many of you know our nation is in sin? Proverbs 14:34 says, "Righteousness exalts a nation, but sin is a disgrace to any people." Can God's Word speak to our personal problems? Think about this: "But seek first the kingdom of God and His righteousness, and all these things will be given to you as well."

Now, listen for a moment to 2 Chronicles 7:14: "If My people, who are called by My name, shall humble themselves..." How many of you know the church needs to humble itself? We need humility before God. I'm calling the church today. The church can be too proud. The church is not supposed to be led by outstanding people, but by kneeling people—people who are on their knees, praying, and seeking His face. We need to be hungry for God, for lost souls. We need to be hungry for the world to know God. It says to turn from our wicked ways.

When you turn, you don't just turn halfway. Come on. Imagine you're driving, and you come to an intersection. You have a left turn or a right turn. If you turn just halfway, are you going to make it? No, you're not going to make it down that road. That's the problem—many people are turning away from their sin, but they're only turning halfway. They're not fully turning away; they're only halfway there. They won't make the necessary adjustments. We cannot do it halfway. Each one of us must repent, confess, be baptized, and be revived.

Then it says, after all this, "Then I will hear from heaven and will forgive their sin and heal their land." Our nation has a lot of work to do. Come on, our nation has a lot of work to do.

They can blame Trump, the media, Hillary, Republicans, Democrats, dead people, or live people. They can blame race, racism, or anything and everything. But let me tell you something: that's not turning away from sin. That's not repentance. That's not confessing our sins. Our nation needs to confess its sins. Abortion alone has brought a great deal of sin upon our nation.

People say they should have a choice, their own choice. I understand that if a woman is raped, there's nothing in this world that would make her want to carry a rapist's baby. I get that. But the problem is that when you open the door just a little bit, you're also opening it for a 16-year-old who just wants to have fun, get pregnant, and have an abortion whenever she wants.

It's gotten to the point where our government legalized abortion for a 16-year-old. Let me tell you something, that law is about to change. That's one of the changes Trump wants to make, and I give praise to God for that. Because no 16-year-old truly understands the gravity of what they're doing when they're trying to end a life in their womb.

Sure, they shouldn't be having sex at that age anyway, but that's the reality of the world we live in. Our nation needs to turn away from these things. We need to start shutting the door on certain behaviors. Some say the government should have no say in what a woman does with her body. But let me tell you, it's not really about the woman's body—it's about the life inside that body.

Another issue that's not getting enough attention is assisted suicide. It's been legalized, and doctors can now give you a pill to end your life. When Dr. Kevorkian did something like that, it was a huge controversy. People were outraged, and he was prosecuted. But we don't live in the same world anymore. Our nation needs to turn away from these practices. You can't do it halfway. You can't say, "Let's give people a choice here, but not there." You can't label it one way for one group and differently for another.

This isn't about politics—it's about our nation. Our nation should stand firm on God's principles, regardless of what politics says. It should stand firmly enough in the things of God to know that abortion is wrong. It wouldn't matter if abortion was legalized; if our nation didn't want to do it, we wouldn't do it. The problem is, the more it's legalized, the more people are doing it—even Christians. Why? Because no one is preaching that it's wrong. Everyone's trying to be politically correct. But God says, "Turn from your wicked ways, humble yourselves, and I will heal your land."

Our nation has a lot of work to do. Some people are talking about how much Trump is going to fail, but let me tell you something—it's not about Trump. Our nation is so messed up right now that it wouldn't matter if we had twelve people in the White House working as President simultaneously. It wouldn't be enough to fix what has happened to our nation over the last 25 or 30 years. Both Republicans and Democrats have contributed to the mess we're in. But God will bring revival to our land and to our people, the church, if we humble ourselves, pray, and turn from our wicked ways.

It's time for revival. But with revival comes responsibility. You might have to pray for five minutes a day. You might worry about falling behind, but we have to get to the point where we make prayer a priority.

Let me tell you something about priorities. Daily prayer is a priority for me. I don't have to be obnoxious about it. I can pray when I'm by myself, in the bathroom, or sitting at my desk waiting for the computer to do something. I pray several times a day. Another daily priority is brushing my teeth—something I do every day, not just once in a while. I'm saying this for a reason. Showering is usually on that list too, along with changing underwear. You might wonder why I'm saying this, but I want to give you a visual aid. These are things we do every day.

If we can do simple things like brushing our teeth every day, we can also pray every day. The problem is, some people around here are having a hard time with that. Some people started strong, but then they realized how much work it is to do it every day, and they gave up.

We get to the point where we do certain things every day, and that's the point I want to make. Imagine replacing TV time with prayer, or brushing your teeth before watching TV. What if, before you could touch your phone, you had to pray? It's about making prayer a daily habit.

We need to humble ourselves and turn from our wicked ways. It's a simple plan, but it requires daily commitment, just like brushing your teeth or taking a shower. You don't forget to do those things because they're important. How many of you have ever said you "forgot" to pray? Most of the time, it's not that you forgot; you just chose not to do it.

When you're lying in bed at night and a parent comes upstairs, can you honestly say you forgot to brush your teeth? No, you just didn't do it. Let's move on to the next point. Today, let's look at God's visual aid. Ezekiel was a man of God, confronted with the congregation of God's people. That's what the dry bones represent—people who are discouraged, displaced, and spiritually dead. The circumstances were ripe for revival.

Let me tell you, the church right now as a whole has never been as spiritually dead as it is today. For example, most people who went to the Lakeland revival are spiritually dead right now. Most people who attended the Litchfield revival are spiritually dead too. Even in Belleville, many were spiritually dead even when revival was happening. So how much more dead do you think they are now?

God took Ezekiel to a mountaintop and gave him a visual aid of revival. God showed him what He wanted to do—He wanted to resurrect His people, to breathe life back into them, and to raise them up as a mighty army.

This means they once lived, and God is going to raise up a church that once lived. But where is He going to do that? In dead religion. The only way to reach the church right now is to break through that dead old religion.

People who were once in revival are now smoking pot. They're having sex with multiple partners. They're sitting around smoking cigarettes, drinking alcohol, getting drunk, and having parties—and still thinking they're fine with God. But let me tell you something:

they're dead, dried up. Revival is about bringing back to life what was once alive but is now dead. Can these bones live again? God asked that very question—can these bones live again? I believe that's what God is asking the church right now. There are several churches right here in town, and God is saying, "Can these bones live again?"

Ezekiel obeyed God and preached to those dry bones, and then God breathed life into them—He brought His Spirit back into those bodies. God revived a mighty army for Himself. But today's churches are full of people, yet many are empty in the eyes of God. Thank you. Come on. There are a lot of people, and many churches are full—but not here, and not in other places. They've filled up with people, but there's no God there.

Too many of God's people have a self-sufficient spirit. Come on. I like to call it an apathetic spirit, or as I like to say, a "pathetic spirit." It's a dead, disobedient lifestyle. Disobedient. So, can these bones live again? That's the question. Don't you think it's interesting that God asked Ezekiel, "Can these bones live?" Don't you think God already knew the answer? That's what God is asking us today—can these bones live? He's asking us right now, "Can these bones live again?"

Why is it that more people are coming to church, but they're experiencing less? They haven't confessed their sins. They are spiritual corpses—dry bones. Come on, get a visual. Imagine the nearest cemetery, and every person buried there was placed in our seats. Some have been dead a long time, some only a short time, but all of them are decayed and dead. We just get as many to fill up the house as we can. That's what religion looks like—a handful of people who love God, who are present in God, who are seeking God, and the rest are dead. The rest are dry. The rest have no life flowing through them anymore. They are decaying and rotting right before our very eyes.

Whoo! Come on. I wish you could see it. Some of you might want to turn around and just get the visual. Because the ocean is out behind us, and there are a lot more seats there. Come on. Dry bones. I'm not talking about the clean skeletons they have in science class or at the doctor's office. I'm talking about the ones that still have dead flesh on them. Some are completely dead, completely dry, but they're still just lying there, with bugs still flying around them. Nasty. But that's what the church looks like.

The pastor preaches, and he's wondering why nothing changes. Why? Because, first of all, God is asking that man or woman, "Can these bones live?" And they're not responding. Why? Because it's too much against their agenda. It's too much against being politically correct. It's too much about just staying in their little party of a private assembly. But let me tell you something—it's not about the assembly here. It's about the assembly out there. And if we don't get the church resurrected right now, if the church doesn't come alive, if these corpses don't live, we're not going to see the movement that God has promised.

We're not going to see the world turned upside down. We're not going to see the people who burn the American flag find Jesus. Because they're dry. And guess what? If the church is dead, the world will die. If the church is dead, the world will die. The world's not going to save itself. The church has to live first for the world to find Jesus.

Spiritual corpses—dry bones. How do you know if bones are getting dry? How do you know? Here are some examples, some points. Are you ready?

Number one: When people have no desire to read the Bible or pray, they're dry bones. Some of this should sting a little. No desire to pray or read the Bible. Aren't you excited?

Number two: When spiritual conversations embarrass you, or you avoid them. In other words, when someone starts talking about God, you just want to tune out. They start talking about the things of God, and you're just trying to shut the conversation down because you don't like where it's going. I don't know. I've seen that somewhere before. Aren't you excited?

Let me stay on that for a second. Spiritual conversations and discussions about the things of God should set us on fire, should stir us up a bit. I remember coming back from revival meetings, and just talking about it got us all stirred up again. Even after the services, we had revival just talking about what happened. Only those who were dry bones wanted to leave early. Remember that? Isn't it funny?

Number three: When you rationalize your sin. Anyone try to convince themselves their sin is okay? Here's an example: "It was just a white lie." Come on, hallelujah. There are no levels of lies. The Bible says all liars shall burn in the lake of fire—all of them. Come on, we try to rationalize it, try to convince ourselves it's alright to sin just this once. Come on. Aren't you excited? Should we stay here for a minute?

Keep talking. Stir some people up. You know, sometimes we get angry about something, we get stirred up. The Bible talks about being angry, but sin not. See, the problem isn't getting mad—it's how you hold on to that anger.

If anger turns into bitterness, it becomes sin. God knew we'd get angry, but it's the part about "sin not" that we need to focus on. You can't hold onto that anger. It makes me so mad—well, get over it. We have to get over it. Why? Because holding onto it leads to unforgiveness, and how many of you know that's a sin? We try to rationalize it, saying, "I don't want to forgive them." But you forgive them so that your Heavenly Father can forgive you. That's just how it is, whether you like it or not. Forgive them anyway.

Number four: When you can quote Scripture and attend service, but it makes no difference in your life—that's a sign of being spiritually dry. You might know the Word, but without any change or fruit in your life, it's just words. How many know people who can preach the Word but have no spirit? That's a fruitless Christianity. It's dry bones. We've got to keep preaching before these people return to their spiritual caskets.

Number five: When your life revolves around money, you're drying up. The enemy wants you so consumed by it that even if you say, "I know God will provide," you forget the little blessings because you're too focused on money. That's dry bones.

Number six: When it no longer bothers you that others are in misery or spiritually lost. If you can see someone who's lost, someone who's going through severe struggles, and it doesn't bother you at all, your bones are drying up. Our nation, especially the church, is funny that way. We'll show compassion for a limping dog, but we'll ignore a person who's been through a life of abuse and hardship, someone who might have just crawled out of a dumpster, and we feel nothing for them. But the Bible says we're supposed to care for the widows, the orphans, and those in need.

God spoke to me not too long ago about how many homeless people in America are former military. They fought for our country, lost everything—family, friends, their sanity—and our government didn't do right by them. They made it so hard for these veterans that now they're just lying out there. Our government offers benefits, but it's like pulling teeth to get them. Even VA hospitals just want to reject them and rush them in and out.

That's spiritually lost, people in misery. It's messed up that our country rejects those who defended it while others get rich off politics. People become millionaires and billionaires through political gains, while those who served in wars are dying on the streets. I don't know about you, but I have compassion for people. That doesn't mean we have to witness to everyone. It was easier for me to witness to someone on the street when I was on my own, but now with a family, it's different.

But that's what dries up the church—the lack of compassion for the lost and the dying. Here's another example: someone comes into church smelling like alcohol, and the church rejects them. Hey, they came to church! I don't care if they smell terrible, like they just crawled out of a dumpster or a winery. They came to the right place. But the church is drying up because it's forgotten what it's for.

Number seven: When worship and service to God no longer excite you, you're drying up. Sometimes we're tired and dry, just dying on the vine, and then we show up to church, start worshiping, and after a few minutes, that rhythm comes back. Worship should excite you. If it doesn't, it means you're dying. How do you get it back? Worship more.

Number eight: When you no longer have the blessing of assurance. We should be assured that God is our Savior. Let's look closer at these dry bones. Is the church suffering from the effects of modern society? I believe it is, because the church is ignoring what's happening outside its walls. I don't know about you, but the church should have been in more of an uproar when the White House was lit up in rainbow colors. The church is drying up because it's been in a desert place—no rain, no water.

Has the church been torn apart in battle? I believe some people start to dry up spiritually because they've been through battles and lost. My wife and I have said many times in our private conversations, it's no wonder more Christians don't go where we go. It's tough sometimes, not always easy. The hardest part is our flesh. But when you're in the storm, it feels like it'll last forever, doesn't it?

Have you ever gone through a test and felt like it would never end? Some of you might be in that place right now. I said this not too long ago: the hardest thing we're dealing with right now is waiting. It's not hardship, difficulty, or opposition—it's waiting. One of the worst places to wait is at the dentist. You sit there in pain, waiting for relief, and even after they numb you up, you're still waiting for the procedure to be done.

Waiting feels like that sometimes. You're just sitting there, in pain, waiting for something to happen. But remember, the battle of waiting can be tough, but it's necessary.

And see, the church gives up. They wither and die because they've been waiting so long that they finally give up on the wait. But here's a promise: Just like waiting for the right moment or the right person, like waiting for my wife, it will always be worth the wait.

Come on, it's like that moment when everything finally clicks—cha-ching! Even if you've made mistakes before, strike one, strike two, strike three—you keep going because it's worth it.

The church has been torn apart in battle, and now we find ourselves wondering where everyone has gone. That could be a sign of dry bones. We sit here and go through the names: this one's gone, that one's gone. When you start counting on your fingers and toes, it can make you feel dry, worried about those who have left.

But you know what? It used to bother me, but now I'm more like, "Hey, they're gone? See ya, bye!" It's not our job to keep everyone. It's not about keeping a graveyard of Christians—people who are physically present but spiritually dead. Sometimes, I feel like we need to go into the church, lift people's hands up, and encourage them to keep going.

When we get to a hopeless state, that's when people dry up and die. Do the problems in the church seem so overwhelming that you don't know where to begin? That's a sign of withering. When you look at the church situation and think, "This is too much," you might be drying up.

In our minds, if we're almost ready to give up on the church, that means we're drying up. But let's flip the script—can these bones live again? That's the question. Revival comes through preaching the Word, the Word that is His. It says to prophesy to the bones. Preaching isn't just about delivering a sermon; it's about sharing what God is saying right now.

If God doesn't tell me something to say, I'm not going to say it. There's no point in just filling time with words. It wasn't in Ezekiel's power, but in the power of the Word of God that came forth. Man doesn't live by bread alone, but by every word that comes from the mouth of God.

The church stops prophesying, stops preaching, stops sharing what God is saying, and that's when we dry up. Revival comes through prayer—we need prayer. In the face of the greatest discouragement, as Matthew Henry said, those who follow God's commands need not doubt success, for God will bless His own plans.

The dry bones came to life when Ezekiel obeyed God's command. The church may seem dried up, but if we obey God's Word, it will live again. God will speak to a man of God, and in the middle of a dead church, life will return, and they will become new.

It's not just about getting people to come to church or revival; it's about igniting a fire within them, helping them realize that they've died on the vine.

I've shared before how, especially in Litchfield, when religious people showed up with arrogance and dryness, they'd fill up an entire section, fold their arms, and challenge us to show them something. But God would send me down that aisle, and I'd just touch the one on the end, and the whole row would fall out on the floor.

They were dried up and dying, but I spoke to that dryness, and it came to life—they rose up as a mighty army. Even dead bones, dry bones, move when God calls them to hear His Word.

God will tell the dry bones to listen, and they don't have a choice. Some of these dry bones will hear the Word from unexpected sources—from a tattooed preacher, a guy with a Mohawk, or a woman preacher.

We almost had a woman in the White House, and we will someday—not Hillary, not Michelle, but someone else. How can we be revived? By recognizing our dryness. No one will be revived if they don't first recognize that they're dry.

People may say their church is fine, but if the church is stinking and dead, it's not fine. We have to recognize our dryness. If people aren't excited, if they're not getting stirred up, then something's wrong.

Some of us have lost our excitement, but in the last few days, there's been a shift in the atmosphere. We're now on the road to revival, and as we begin to shift in that direction, we can be revived so that we can revive a nation.

Come on, another step toward this is a ruthless confession of sin. We cannot be right without God. Our salvation should be something we rejoice in—something we're thankful for. God has saved me from so much. Walking home from a party, drunk and high, so out of it that I couldn't see where I was going, I staggered into an old building and passed out. The next morning, I woke up surrounded by rats the size of cats. My body ached, but I still moved quickly. As I walked down the street to my hotel, my head felt like it weighed 4,000 pounds.

It's moments like that where I know God saved me from much. He saved me from all kinds of things. Sometimes, kids get frustrated and ask, "Why can't I do this? Why can't I do that?" They don't know what's out there, and I don't want them to. I don't want them to see the things I've seen—blood pouring from a man's body, a woman being assaulted while too unconscious to help. I don't want them to witness torture, molestation, or any of that. They need to know that their God is real and that He's bringing life to this nation.

I'm telling you, a revival is coming, and it's going to start with the body of Christ. It's not just for us, but for the generations to come. Our children need revival in this nation. If anything, we should be out there in our nation, declaring that we need revival. It doesn't matter who's president—we need revival. We can't go around saying, "He's not my president." If you're in America, he is.

It's so frustrating to hear people say, "He's not my president." I didn't vote for Bill Clinton, but guess what? He was my president, even after all the scandals. I didn't vote for him the second time either, but I didn't go out picketing, saying, "He's not my president."

People get so caught up in things. We need to focus on what really matters. How about marching through downtown New York, declaring that we need revival? We need revival in this land, for the youth, for the young people of America. We need revival in our nation right now. We need revival because the nations of the world need revival.

I'm telling you, that's what's going to change things. Nothing else will change it, but Jesus Christ will change the nation.

Hallelujah. People say things like, "We should get rid of the electoral college and just go with the popular vote," because they lost and want to change the laws. But when a nation has a democracy, we need to stand behind it. The Word of God says it's a sin to go against the government. We're supposed to honor the law of the land—that's what the Bible says.

There's a lot of hypocrisy in our nation. Political figures have gained power for themselves while rejecting the needs of the people.

Billions of dollars were sent to help places like Haiti, but the people there barely got anything—maybe a bowl of rice, if they were lucky. We live in a world that's dying, a world that's going to hell, and our nation has helped many, even when it's been crumbling.

We need to understand that change is coming, but it's going to come through fire—true fire. Fire is going to come upon the youth and the young people. Fire will cause the dry bones to live again. Fire will bring life back. God says there's a 10-year span of the Spirit and power of revival that's supposed to happen, and it's already started. We need to thank God because it's coming now.

Some of you have asked God to take you out of distractions, to not let you be consumed by them, so you can give Him more time. Why? It's not always for you, but for the people you're going to reach for God, the people you're going to touch for Him.

People don't realize heaven and hell are real. I'll share a small part of a story—I don't want to tell the whole thing. No matter how many times I've known heaven or hell is real, there was a time when I laid hands on a man, and the moment I touched his head, I felt the agony of suffering. God said he was already in hell, already dead and in hell. When I felt that, I disconnected as fast as I could. It was a feeling I can't fully explain, but it was worse than dry bones.

It felt like dry bones, like a decayed skeleton out of the casket, rotting flesh being consumed by the pit of hell. That experience changed the way I feel and the way I see things because we live in a different world than we used to.

God is coming soon. Hallelujah. We need revival. We need revival. We need our lives stirred up, our prayer lives stirred up. We need revival. Are you ready?

We give you praise.

About the Author

Diving deep into the realms of spiritual awakening, Bill Vincent embodies a connection with the Supernatural that spans over three decades. With a robust prophetic anointing, he has dedicated his life to ministry, serving as a guiding light and a pillar of strength in Revival Waves of Glory Ministries.

Bill Vincent is not just a Minister but a prolific Author, contributing to the spiritual enlightenment of many through his diverse range of writings and teachings. His work encompasses themes of deliverance, fostering the presence of God, and shaping Apostolic, cutting-edge Church structure. His insights are drawn from a wellspring of experience, steeped in Revival, and fine-tuned by a profound Spiritual Sensitivity.

In his relentless pursuit of God's Presence and his commitment to sustaining Revival, Bill focuses primarily on inviting divine encounters and maintaining a spiritual atmosphere ripe for transformation. His extensive library of over 125 books serves as a beacon of hope, guiding countless individuals in overcoming the shackles of Satan and embracing the light of God.

Revival Waves of Glory Ministries is not your typical church – it's a prophetic ministry, a sanctuary where the Holy Spirit is given the freedom to move as He wills. Our sermons, a blend of divine wisdom and revelation, can be experienced on Rumble, immersing you in the transformative power of the Word: https://rumble.com/c/revivalwavesofgloryministriesbillvincent

For a deeper exploration into our teachings, visions, and the manifold grace of God, visit https://www.revivalwavesofgloryministries.com/.

Embark on a journey of spiritual discovery with Bill Vincent, and let the waves of revival wash over you, unveiling the divine power and boundless love of God!

Podcast: https://podcasters.spotify.com/pod/show/bill-vincent2

Rumble: https://rumble.com/c/revivalwavesofgloryministriesbillvincent

Be sure to check out our new videos **Downloads From Heaven!**

Donate: https://www.revivalwavesofgloryministries.com/giving

Bookstore: https://www.revivalwavesofgloryministries.com/online-stores

Invite Bill Vincent (PREACH, TEACH AND PROPHETIC MINISTRY) to your Event: rwgministry@yahoo.com

Milton Keynes UK
Ingram Content Group UK Ltd.
UKHW040117021124
450424UK00005BC/805